THE TALE OF KING HARALD

Thomas J.T. Williams has asserted his right to be identified as the author of this work.

First published in 2014 by The British Museum Press
A division of The British Museum Company Ltd
38 Russell Square, London WC1B 3QQ

britishmuseum.org/publishing

A catalogue reference for this book is available from the British Library

ISBN 978-0-7141-2344-8

Additional object detail illustrations on pages 22–3, 40–1, 58–9, 80–1 and 108–9 by William Webb
Designed by James Alexander at JADE Design
Printed in Spain by Grafos SA, Barcelona

Contents

SWED

SI

Stiklestad

NORWAY

SHETLAND

ORKNEY

OSLO

ROSKILDE

DENMARK

YORK
Stamford Bridge

ENGLAND

SIC

CHAPTER I

Flight

 ONG AGO, *in the days when dragons could still be found and fought (or so it is written in the tales of those times), there lived a* Viking king. *He was fierce and warlike, brave and strong, cunning and cruel. His name was Harald Hard-ruler and that name was feared wherever it was heard.*

But it was not always so . . .

This tale begins when Harald was still a boy. Fifteen years old, he had awoken alone, deep in the dark forest, and wounded near to death.

The forest was full of terrors: there were wolves and bears, and more dreadful things too it was said. Harald had listened as a child to the stories told by the skalds, the poets who recited ancient tales in the halls of wealthy chiefs. They sung of dreadful magics and the wakeful dead, of giants and trolls and foul dwellers in inky bogs. Harald had never thought much about such things. But now, as he looked into the black spaces between the trunks of the silent trees, wounded and afraid, those tales came back to him and filled him up with fear. He reached for the cross around his neck and wondered whether God would protect him, the God his half-brother had fought and died for.

Harald's half-brother, King Olaf, had always been a grim and ruthless man. He had tried to stamp his religion and his rule on all of Norway. But he had loved Harald. He would often tell the story of how, when he had tried to frighten the little boy, Harald would stare back at him insolently, unblinking. And once, when he had tweaked a hair on Harald's head, the child had reached up and tugged on his whiskers.

Olaf would roar with laughter when he told that story: 'You'll be vengeful one day, my friend,' he would say.

It was at a place called Stiklestad that Olaf met his end. The farmers of Norway had rebelled against his rule and his religion, and had come to meet him in battle, hoping to drive him out and bring back their old ways and their old kings. 'Forward, forward, peasant farmers!' they had shouted as they marched into battle.

Bishop Sigurd was with them. He worked for Cnut, the great king who had ruled over England and Denmark, as well as Norway for a time – until Olaf returned to reclaim the Norwegian throne for himself. Sigurd urged the farmers on: 'Advance and cast these sinners to the wolves and eagles; leave the corpses where they lie,' he said fiercely.

But many of the rebels were not Christians. Harald had seen the war-witches casting spells for blades to be sharpened and armour to be hardened. They yelled and danced and brandished their staffs from among the battle lines. Some of the warriors howled like wolves as they rushed into combat – they felt the power of wild beasts surging within them and thought nothing of their own safety. Harald liked that. He thought men should always face death without fear.

Olaf had showed no fear – save only for his little brother Harald.

'I think it would be best', he said, 'if my brother doesn't fight in this battle; he's still only a child.'

But Harald would have none of it.

'I shall be in the fight,' he said.

'I'm not so puny that I can't handle a weapon; I might even tie the hilt of my sword to my hand. I'm keener than anyone to give these farmers a good thrashing.'

And so they went into battle together.

Olaf looked
magnificent
that day. His shield
was painted white, with
a gold cross inlaid, and in his
hand he carried a great spear. His
helmet too was decorated with gold and
he was protected by a shining coat of chain
mail that gleamed in the sun. At his belt he
wore his sword, the hilt cunningly wrought with
gold and silver wire. The sword was named
Hneiter – which means 'cutter' – and it was a
famous blade.

Before him was carried his banner, a cloth
of white upon which a great serpent was
depicted – twisted and tangled and
writhing. It would be hard to

imagine a mightier or more glorious king. But soon the light began to dim and the sky turned blood red. Before long the sun had disappeared and the world was plunged into darkness, even though it was the middle of the day. It seemed a terrible omen of what was to come and so it proved to be.

The fighting lasted many hours and Olaf fought like a hero of old. He stood in the front rank, raining blows down on his enemies. Few of his foes could bear to look at him, so fearsome did he seem to them, and many ran away rather than face that dreadful sword. But, as the darkness of the day thickened, so the tide of battle slowly turned against him and in the end he fell, struck down by many wounds, at the great stone that stood on the battlefield.

Harald could not remember what else had happened. All was a whirling confusion of running and shouting, noise and blood. He remembered a strong hand on his shoulder and a swift flight. He remembered the sight of his own blood on his clothes and realized he'd been hurt. But he did not know how he had come to be in the forest.

And now he was not alone.

Up ahead a tall figure was approaching, moving stealthily through the gloom. What nightmare was this? A troll from the north come down to gnaw his bones? Harald felt panic surge through his limbs. His wounds forgotten, he turned to run … but slipped, falling to the damp sea of pine needles that covered the ground.

'Ho, little prince!' came a familiar voice. 'You're awake! That is good news indeed … I'm weary of carrying you like a sack of logs.'

Harald felt a wave of relief that brought tears to his eyes: it was Rögnvald Brusason. Rögnvald was the son of the

Earl of Orkney, and had come to live at the court of King Olaf a year before the battle. He and Harald had become firm friends, even though Rögnvald was a good deal older than Harald. It must have been he who had helped him to escape from Stiklestad.

'I've been searching out the path ahead – now that you're up and about we'd better get going. Come along, lazybones!'

Rögnvald was a fine Viking – tall, handsome, strong and golden-haired. He was a fortunate companion for a journey in dark places, good-humoured and quick to laugh, but also resourceful and a skilful hunter. In time Rögnvald would become a powerful man and rule as an Earl of Orkney with his uncle, Thorfinn the Mighty. But that's a tale for another time.

Rögnvald knew of a farmhouse where Harald could heal his wounds, and it was there they headed through that terrible wood. They journeyed for many days, scrambling down into deep ravines and climbing over rocky hillsides dank with moss. Often Harald had to be held upright as the pain in his side grew worse. During the day they'd travel slowly, following the trail that Rögnvald found for them, always anxious for signs of pursuers. At night it was worse. Many times it was too damp to light a fire, and they'd huddle among the roots of trees and shudder at the sound of the wolves howling in the mountains. The nights last a long time in the north and it was a grim journey.

At last they found the house that Rögnvald had spoken of and just in time, for Harald had grown very weak. They were received well by the farmer and his wife, for in those days it was considered the worst discourtesy of all to deny food and shelter to weary travellers.

So Harald ate meat and drank beer, and sat by the warmth of the fire until his fears had left him and the pain of his wounds began to lessen. It wasn't long before he felt strong again, but there was no going back home. Cnut's men would be looking for him, hoping to finish him off, and he only had Rögnvald to protect him. He also had a grim task ahead that he knew he must carry out. King Olaf had a son – Magnus – and now Harald would have to tell him that his father was dead.

And so it was that the two fugitives set out again, once more into the forests and on into the lands of the Svear (as the people of Sweden were called in those days). Rögnvald went first, travelling ahead to meet up with other survivors and supporters of King Olaf. Harald followed on horseback, hooded and cloaked, guided by the farmer's son. No one knew that he was a royal prince, and he began to think more often about the terrible fate that had befallen them after the battle.

One day, sitting on a tree stump, he made up a verse:

'Now I pass from wood to wood,
A wanderer of little worth;
Who knows? My name may yet be
Known far and wide hereafter.'

The guide looked at Harald strangely, but said nothing.

Eventually they came to the hall of the Swedish king, Anund Jacob, in the town of Sigtuna, nestled on the shores of Lake Mälaren. The farmer's son turned for home, but not before he was presented with lavish gifts of furs and a great silver arm-ring. He knew then that this hooded stranger must be an important person to have such rich and powerful friends. As he rode back through the woods, he thought of the verse the boy had recited and wondered whether he would ever know the stranger's name.

Harald was cheered to find Rögnvald waiting for him with a troop of warriors, all survivors of the battle. He began to hope that maybe the future would not be as bleak as it had seemed since Stiklestad. As they sat in the hall of the Swedish king, feasting on roasted game and mead, he listened to the skalds singing tales of ancient gods and heroes in the flickering firelight. For a moment he forgot where he was and imagined himself back in Norway again – a prince at the high table of King Olaf.

But then he felt a lurch in his stomach and the pain of his wound, and remembered the battle and his brother's fall. And he remembered too the journey that still lay ahead – to his nephew Magnus, far to the east, in the snowy lands of the Rūs.

Viking belief

At the time of the Battle of Stiklestad in 1030, many people in Scandinavia were Christian. However, becoming Christian did not mean that the old gods were forgotten – many people remembered the stories and beliefs of their ancestors. In some places it took much longer for the people to convert to Christianity, especially in remote parts of Norway and Sweden. Before becoming Christian, Vikings made sacrifices to the gods at sacred places in the landscape. Some of those gods were powerful and well-known. Odin, god of war and magic, and Thor, god of thunder, were popular, but many lesser gods and goddesses are forgotten.

This cross was raised on the Isle of Man by a man called Thorwald. It shows Odin being swallowed by the giant wolf Fenrir in the battle at the end of the world (*Ragnarok*).

This is an axe with a section cut out of the middle to make the shape of a cross. Becoming Christian did not mean becoming peaceful. Christian Vikings were just as warlike as their pagan ancestors.

This crucifix would have been worn around the neck of a Viking. It was made in Scandinavia and would have made it clear that the wearer was a Christian.

This amulet shows Odin sitting on his throne. He wears female clothing because the sorcery he practised was normally carried out by women. The ravens either side of him are called *Hugin* (thought) and *Munin* (memory).

Thor used his hammer *Mjolnir* to fight the giants who threatened the realm of the gods (*Asgard*). This pendant in the shape of a hammer has also been decorated with a cross, and its owner may have worshipped Thor and Christ at the same time.

CHAPTER 2

Exile

EYOND SIGTUNA *and the waters of Lake Mälaren lay the ocean, and further still was the land that the Vikings knew as Gardariki, from where the great rivers flowed and merchants brought great hoards of silver back from the east. This was the road that lay before Harald and Rögnvald. King Anund had bought them passage on a merchant vessel that was heading for the lands of the Rūs. The captain had agreed to transport the men and their provisions to the trading post at Staraya Ladoga, where he would stock up with furs and amber for the journey south.*

The ship was small and fat. Harald wished he was on board a great warship like the ones the Swedish king had moored at Sigtuna, or like the mighty vessel his brother Olaf had built. That had been a magnificent dragon-ship, long, narrow and fast, with forty pairs of oars to drive it over the waves. Harald wondered what had happened to it.

'One day I'll build ships like that,' he muttered sulkily, as he sat huddled on the deck of the trading boat.

The way was long. First they sailed through a strange land made of hundreds of tiny islands and narrow straits. Harald had to admire the captain's skill at navigating his way through such a dangerous sea-road. But after a while they came to broader waters, and for several days steered a course to the east. Sometimes Harald would sit at the back of the ship, taking charge of the great steering oar that held the ship to its course, but there was little else for him to do. Every day the rising sun appeared against the prow of the ship on its journey.

Before long they came close to land again. To the north

they could see a dark shoreline, thick with forest. Small islands and bays were dotted here and there.

'That's the land of the Cwenas,' the captain told them. 'They're strange folk. I've heard it told that they have very small boats that they carry around on their backs.' Harald wasn't sure if he believed him. The captain was called Einar One-eye. He was a big Gotlander, full of tall tales about dog-headed men and monsters with their faces on their chests. But from the number of silver rings he wore around his arms he was clearly a successful businessman, whatever nonsense he talked, and Harald believed him when he said that he'd once been a fierce Viking raider – his face and arms bore the scars of many wounds.

Eventually they reached a place where the sea ended and the forest became the horizon.

'What now?' exclaimed Harald. 'How are we supposed to carry on? We don't have horses or enough provisions for a long overland journey.'

Einar gave a great laugh. 'We won't need to go on foot,

little warrior. See over there,
that line of silver cutting the
horizon? That's the River Neva.
We shall sail up there as easily as we
sailed across the wide sea … all the way to
Lake Ladoga!'

As they entered the mouth of the Neva, it was
at first no different to being at sea, but, as they
sailed on, the river narrowed, and it seemed
that the forests on either
side became thicker

and darker with every mile. As the light began to dim, Harald began to feel a prickling on his skin and the hairs on his neck standing on end. Soon it was too dark to navigate and they were forced to drop anchor in the middle of the river.

That night Harald didn't sleep. Wolves were howling deep in the woods, and he was convinced that he could hear even stranger sounds – drums and weird voices from the darkness beyond the water. Once he was convinced he saw an orange burst of flame, but it was gone in an instant. In the morning he asked Rögnvald if he'd seen anything.

'Nothing, little prince,' he said. 'I slept like a bear in winter.'

There were no more strange sounds the following day and it wasn't long before they emerged into the vast waters of Lake Ladoga. They sailed close to the shore as they followed the lake round to the east, and there – to the south – was their first destination: Staraya Ladoga.

It was a bustling little town with people shouting in many different tongues. Everywhere Harald looked there were barrels being loaded and unloaded, and here and there men haggled over the price of beads, furs, amber and great balls of wax. A man dressed head to toe in furs was arguing loudly with a fellow dressed in enormous silk trousers whose arms were weighed down with silver arm-rings.

Harald thought he looked absurd, but he was clearly a very wealthy man. The young prince couldn't understand what they were talking about because the fur-clad man spoke in a language Harald hadn't heard before. The dispute seemed to be about silver: the furry man was pointing furiously at a set of hanging scales on a nearby table. In one dish sat a handful of what looked like dice, in the other some bars of silver bullion.

Einar saw Harald watching the men.

'The man in furs is a trapper,' Einar told him. 'He's angry because he thinks he's being cheated in payment for the marten skins that Leifr there is trying to buy from him.

Those things like dice are his weights – he bought them from Arab merchants in the South. The dots tell him how heavy each weight should be.'

'Why does the trapper think that he's being cheated?' asked Harald.

'Ha! Because the trapper has his own weights and they tell him something different. They'll have to start again now and work out a different system. This is how it always goes. But Leifr is a crook – he uses lighter weights when he's buying and heavy ones when selling.'

Harald looked at the two men again. Now they were comparing each other's weights in the scales, trying to reach a compromise. He was sure he saw the merchant slipping new weights from a pouch on to the scales when the other man wasn't looking. Harald decided he didn't like Leifr or his ridiculous baggy trousers.

It wasn't long before they were on the move again. Einar had loaded a dozen barrels on to the ship, as well as a number of wooden boxes. He told Harald they were full of 'all sorts of things that will fetch a good price – amber mostly: I've been stockpiling at Ladoga all year'.

This time they were travelling south. The ship sat lower in the water now and the crew had to work hard at the oars. After a few days they saw a town rising on the western shore. It was big, far bigger than Staraya Ladoga, bigger even than Sigtuna and the places in Norway Harald had known as a boy. He stood in the prow of the ship, amazed by the high wooden gables and the domes of the churches rising above them.

'Welcome to Novgorod!' shouted Einar.

There was little time for goodbyes. Harald and Rögnvald were met at a small jetty by a warrior in a helmet and leather armour. He escorted them quickly away from the river and into the town, through a maze of narrow streets and wooden walls, until they arrived at a great hall, not unlike that of the Swedish king, but bigger and grander and hung inside with marvellous silk tapestries of amazing quality.

'You like my furnishings?' A strong voice came from a darker part of the hall beyond the fire that burned in the centre of the room. Harald started – his head was still spinning from the swift walk from the jetty. A man stepped into the firelight. He was tall and had a brown beard flecked with silver. His clothes were costly, embroidered and fur-lined, but not foolish like Leifr's giant pantaloons.

'They're from Constantinople, the capital of the Byzantine Empire. The Emperor sent them to me as a gift. But forgive me, I'm being rude. I am Yaroslav, Grand Prince of Novgorod and all the Rūs. Welcome to my house.'

That night Yaroslav hosted a great feast in his halls. There was wine from the south and great slabs of beef and venison. Harald sat back, at last feeling some of the weariness of his long journey leaving him. A skald struck up a strange tune – it was like nothing Harald had ever heard before – filled with the magic of faraway places; but it was familiar too, like meeting a forgotten friend in a strange land. Suddenly a voice began to sing, deep and resonant. The language was one that Harald knew, though the accent was of the east, and it addressed the hall:

'Listen,' it said. 'Listen now, to the tale of bygone years …'

It was Yaroslav who sang.

As Harald listened to the rich voice of the Grand Prince, the firelight flickered on the Byzantine tapestries. And the words danced on the strange melody and lulled him, until he didn't know if he was awake or dreaming, but figures began to move in the shadows on silk and carved wood, and the tale came alive in his mind.

He saw wild tribes battling fiercely among themselves –
the peoples of the Chud, the Krivichi, the Ves, the Slavs
and the Slovenes. Then among them appeared
Rurik, a mighty warrior come down from the
north. All the tribes bent the knee, begging
Rurik and his brothers to rule over
them. And so they did. Hordes
of Vikings came down the rivers
to Ladoga and beyond, founding
Novgorod and raising other towns
with soaring timber palisades …
Harald saw the warlords Askold
and Dir seizing the city of Kiev,
and great Oleg's death at the
fangs of a snake hidden among
the bones of his dead horse.

The names tumbled down the years, like river water over rapids: from Oleg to Igor, from Igor to Sviatoslav, from Sviatoslav to Yaropolk and from Yaropolk to Vladimir. Of Vladimir there were many tales: how he had crushed the Yatvingians and pillaged the Bulgars, of his wives and his fortresses, and of his servants wandering the world – questioning the priests of many faiths – until Vladimir was satisfied and brought the Christianity of Byzantium to the Rūs.

'So you see,' the music had ended and Yaroslav was speaking now and his eyes were on Harald, 'I am descended from great Northmen just as you are. For Vladimir was my father and my line goes back unbroken to Rurik of old. And there it doesn't end, for my wife Ingegerd is a daughter of the old Swedish king Olaf Tribute-king and our children bear the blood of many northern lords.'

The spell was broken and Harald quickly gathered his wits. He realized that Yaroslav was offering a bond of distant kinship as a descendant of noble Vikings and that this was a gesture of goodwill that demanded great

courtesy. Harald knelt before the Grand Prince.

'Great Prince,' he said, 'you do me great honour. I have no gift to give you, much to my shame, but for your hospitality and in respect of the kinship between my people and your family, I offer my service, my loyalty and the strength of my sword arm – such as it is.'

'This I gladly accept!' said Yaroslav warmly. 'And you shall stay with me as my honoured hearth-companion, for I loved your brother and I see you are like him. I shall give you warriors to command and halls as you desire. But first I have a gift for you.'

He presented Harald with a sword, wonderfully made with a hilt engraved with a maze of writhing serpents. It was a kingly gift and Harald knew at that moment that the oath he had made was sealed. He was bound to Yaroslav's service for good or ill, a noble warrior in the household of a mighty lord.

That night Harald lay awake, his head spinning with the events of the day. He thought of Yaroslav's tale. Now, with his mind clear and no music or mead to addle his wits, he wondered whether he believed all he had heard – especially about Rurik and his brothers. It seemed strange to him that any people would beg a foreigner to rule over them or that the tribes could have been so easily subdued. He thought again of the drums in the forest. Reaching over, Harald touched the sword that lay beside him; it was cold and hard in his clammy hand. The wind whispered in the trees outside.

————

The next day Harald was taken to a different hall. There he met Yaroslav's wife, Ingegerd, a beautiful and stately woman, and she introduced Harald to her daughter Elisabeth. The little girl was only five years old and Harald didn't know what to make of her. The child didn't speak; she just stared up at him with huge cow eyes and followed him around the room in silent fascination.

Harald started to feel irritated: he was a noble warrior in the service of a great prince – he didn't want to play with little children. Why had he been brought here? But

Ingegerd led him further into the hall and suddenly he understood. At a bench beside a window sat a young boy of about eleven. He was slight and pale, but his features were familiar because he had his father's eyes. He was Harald's nephew, the son of the dead King Olaf.

'Magnus,' said Harald. The boy looked round, startled.

'Your father is dead, Magnus. Cnut's men killed him, but he died fighting. He was a great warrior.'

The boy said nothing and gazed out of the window. After a while, he turned back to Harald and shrugged.

'I didn't know him. He left me here when I was small. Yaroslav is my father now.'

Harald stared at the pale boy. He didn't know what else to say so he turned his back on him and walked from the hall.

The road to the East

During the Viking Age (from roughly 800 until the time of Harald's adventures), Scandinavian explorers and traders travelled eastwards, down the great rivers of Russia and beyond. They were looking for people to exchange goods with. Amber, furs and other natural resources from the northern world could be traded for silver with the great powers of the east: the Christian Byzantine Empire centred on Constantinople (modern Istanbul) and the states of the Islamic world. Over many generations these Scandinavian adventurers began to settle along the river routes and contributed to the development of a new culture in what is now Russia, Belarus and Ukraine – the Rūs.

Scales such as these were used by Viking traders for weighing quantities of silver and other goods.

Huge numbers of coins with Arabic inscriptions (known as *dirhams*) such as this one have been found in Scandinavia, Russia and Ukraine. They are evidence of contact between Vikings and the Islamic world.

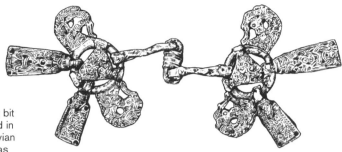

This horse's bit is decorated in a Scandinavian style and was found in Russia.

This coin was minted during the reign of Vladimir the Great, one of the most powerful rulers of the Rūs (see page 35).

These weights were copied from types that Viking traders would have seen in the markets of eastern cities. The number of dots indicates the heaviness of the weight.

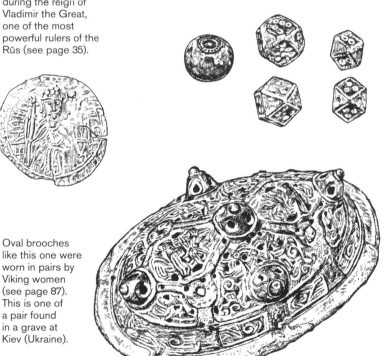

Oval brooches like this one were worn in pairs by Viking women (see page 87). This is one of a pair found in a grave at Kiev (Ukraine).

CHAPTER 3

Adventure

ARALD STAYED *with Yaroslav in Novgorod over that winter. Travel was impossible unless by sledge or skis; sometimes they would organize a hunting party into the dense forests in search of elk and aurochs for their meat, skin and antler. On occasions they would bring back wolf and beaver furs that would later be turned into warm gloves and hats to stave off the fierce northern chill. When the weather was too bad to go abroad, Yaroslav would sit Harald by the fire and teach him words of Greek — 'the language of monks' Yaroslav called it.*

In the spring, when the snows thawed and the rivers became passable, they travelled together by boat to Kiev. On the way the Grand Prince talked endlessly about his plans for monasteries and cathedrals, sometimes gazing into the far distance as he described the glories of far Constantinople.

'You should see it, Harald,' he whispered. 'The soaring golden domes surpass our dreams of heaven, and the walls, with their vast bastions of stone, are like the mountainous walls of Jotunheim, in Utgard where the giants dwell … but these aren't the works of gods or giants, they're the works of men. And men were greater in ages past, Harald, always remember this. We can only struggle to approach the glory of times long gone … but try we must!'

At Kiev, Harald was given men to command and travelled south to the fortresses that Yaroslav had built in his long war against the Pechenegs. The Pechenegs, Yaroslav explained, were a tribe of horsemen from the east who raided from the steppes into the lands of the Rūs and the Byzantine Empire. Their King, Kurya, had treacherously killed Yaroslav's grandfather Sviatoslav and then drunk wine from his empty skull. They were indeed a fearsome people.

Harald was nervous at first. He was still only a young man of sixteen and he was in charge of grown warriors, some twice his age. But he found that, once they knew he was Olaf's brother, they obeyed his commands without question, and he soon began to enjoy the power he had over other men. And he made sure that those who fought well in his service were rewarded with gold and silver.

He quickly learned that from great rewards sprang great loyalty in his followers. Harald also learned skill in battle from men who had spent their whole lives fighting in Yaroslav's wars – veterans of campaigns against the Poles and the Estonians. The sword that had seemed so hard and alien quickly became like a part of his arm. Victories followed swiftly, and with victory came treasure and the loyalty of his war band.

After only a few years, Harald became a respected warlord, feared by the enemies of Yaroslav the Wise.

But he was restless. Despite his skill as a warrior, he had no lands of his own; despite the treasure he had won, he was not as rich as a great prince. But a prince he was, yet in the land of the Rūs there could be no other prince than Yaroslav.

And so it was that one day, when Harald was nearly twenty, he called his closest companions to him and told them of his desire for greater glory, riches and adventure. He asked who would go with him and a great roar went up: he had become a popular leader of men.

'And where shall we go, lord?' asked one of them.

But Harald already knew. The words of Yaroslav still burned in his imagination.

'South. To Byzantium.'

———

Constantinople was like nothing he had ever seen. Even Yaroslav's great cities are like peasant huts in comparison, thought Harald. Nothing, not even the words of the Grand Prince, could have prepared him for the scale, the treasures, the riches of this greatest of cities.

On entering the city, Harald was escorted into the presence of the Emperor Romanos and the Empress Zoe. Their palace was beyond all Harald's imaginings. It was octagonal in plan, with great pillars and arches of coloured marble stacked on top of each other all the way up to the great domed roof. Mosaics of gold and precious stones reared up on all sides – the images of emperors, Christ and the saints looked down from vaults and walls, and music, unlike anything Harald had ever dreamt of, drifted from unseen alcoves.

On all sides were heaps of gold, tables made from rare wood inlaid with precious metals and the priceless relics of saints. The waft of strange incense drifted among the yellow candlelight from great candelabra, making Harald feel as though he had entered into a dream of heaven. Amid all this splendour were two thrones, raised up at the summit of five steps. He knelt before the thrones and a courtier announced him in Greek.

A woman's voice commanded him to rise.

The Empress was looking down at him, smiling. She was much older than Harald and very beautiful.

'And what brings Harald son of Sigurd from beyond the north wind? We have heard much of your exploits, mighty warrior – should we be afraid for our treasures?' The Empress spoke in Greek and her tone was gently mocking, but Harald was hypnotized by her.

'I have come with my men, great lady, to pledge our swords to the Empire and to fight for you – if you will have us.'

The Empress laughed. 'We would be honoured, young prince. You will join the household of my husband's Varangian Guard – the imperial bodyguard of our house – where many of your countrymen already serve us well.'

Harald glanced at the Emperor, who sat in sullen silence. He looked sulky, bored and resentful, and not at all imperial. I'd fight and die for the Empress, thought Harald to himself, but not for this fool Emperor.

Harald had chosen his loyalties wisely. As it turned out, Romanos was dead within the year – strangled, some said, on the orders of the Empress – and Zoe soon had a new husband, the Emperor Michael IV.

This didn't trouble Harald very much. The death of an emperor was an occasion for 'palace plunder' when the new Emperor sought to buy the loyalty of the Varangians by granting them access to the imperial treasury. It was an astonishing sight: heaps of red gold and gemstones filled the marble vaults like the dragon hoards of ancient legend.

Harald filled sacks with treasure that he sent back with trusted men to Yaroslav's court. But, despite the gold and jewels, the death of Romanos made Harald wary, and from that moment onwards he always kept a watchful eye out. The imperial court was a dangerous place to be, and the Empress was like a fire: stray too close to the flame and even the mighty could be burned.

————

Harald didn't stay in the city for long. Soon he was given command of a band of the Varangian Guard and sent far and wide in the service of the Empress and the new Emperor.

Those were the days of Harald's greatest adventures. He fought the Empire's enemies wherever they could be found – and they could be found everywhere. He fought pirates on the Mediterranean Sea and Saracens in Turkey and in Palestine. He captured eighty cities it was said, wandered the ancient streets of Antioch, Damascus and Jerusalem, strode through the ruins of fallen empires and stood with bloody axe raised in triumph on the banks of the great River Euphrates.

In Bulgaria, Harald won his greatest victory, cutting down a rebel king and crushing the Bulgarian uprising. Poets sang his praises and he earned the name 'Bulgar-burner'. In Sicily, Harald fought alongside Norman adventurers. They were hardy warriors descended from Norwegian Vikings like Harald. Their leader, William Iron Arm, was a famous fighter and he and Harald fought side by side for a time. But it wasn't long before they found themselves on opposite sides, and they fought bitterly against each other.

In truth, Harald didn't really care who his enemies were, so long as the gold flowed and his glory grew. And grow it did, until it outshone even the great Byzantine generals. Many stories are told of those times, and none can say what truth is in them, for Harald liked to tell his own tales in later days and no one ever dared to contradict him.

With every victory, Harald's fame spread widely. Hundreds of men flocked to his banner, drawn by the glory of his legend and the wealth that came from success. Most of the men who came were Varangians from the north – Danes, Swedes, Norwegians and Rūs – but Englishmen and Normans came too, and Greeks and Slavs and others from far distant lands. But the warfare was unending. Violence became a way of life for Harald and, as time went on, a change came over him; the fears of his youth were long forgotten and he grew into a hard man – strong and iron-willed, but capable of great bloodshed and betrayal.

One story tells of how Harald pretended to have died in his tent outside the walls of a Sicilian town he was besieging with his army. He lay in a coffin, fully armed, and his men asked the townsfolk if they would allow his

body to be brought in for burial – to which they agreed (they thought the coffin was unusually heavy, not knowing that a man with full armour and weapons lay inside it). But, once inside the town gates, Harald leapt out and killed the bearers, and used the coffin to wedge open the doors. His men rushed into the town and slaughtered the unsuspecting people in their homes, before razing the place to the ground and carrying off its treasures.

It was a cunning deed, but a terrible one, and men began to whisper that Harald had a wicked heart.

In Jerusalem, Harald spoke with priests who told him of the great stain that was growing on his soul on account of all the blood he had spilled. He wasn't worried about the killing – that was how a true Viking won glory – but he was afraid of the fires of hell.

One night he went alone to the tomb of the Holy Sepulchre, where Christ's body had lain when it was taken down from the cross. There he knelt before the altar, praying for forgiveness until the dawn came. But no god spoke to him in that dark crypt, no angelic vision came and no promise of salvation – only darkness, and cold stone, and the thought of devils gathering to take his soul. And in that tomb all the troubles of his childhood came back to Harald.

He thought of the dark forest, and the howling wolves, and his brother lying dead in the mud at Stiklestad with the ravens circling overhead. He shivered and felt the prickle of tears forming. But he gripped his sword hard and shook his head as if to dislodge the demons crowding round him. Olaf would not have sat quivering in the darkness for fear of hellfire, thought Harald. He was a true king of the north. He felt foolish and ashamed, and that in turn made him angry. And so he rose and, turning his back on the altar, he left the tomb of Christ and made his way back to Constantinople.

———

But things had changed in Harald's absence. Walking up the steps to the Imperial Palace, he felt a tension in the air, and saw unfamiliar faces in armour around the door. Something was wrong. Stepping into the chamber and approaching the two thrones, he could see through the fog of incense and candlelight only one figure seated. It wasn't the Emperor Michael IV, nor was it the Empress Zoe.

'What is this!' Harald blurted out. 'Where is the Empress?'

Armoured guards raised their spears and took several steps forward from around the wall of the octagonal throne room. The young man sitting on the throne peered down and spoke in a sneering voice.

'The Empress is banished, Harald Sow's-son. The old Emperor is dead and I, Michael, fifth of that name, now rule. Watch how you address the imperial crown, son of peasants and swineherds.'

Harald drew his sword and his jaw jutted forward defiantly.

'Go to hell, you powdered pup! You are no Emperor and I will not bow the knee to the likes of you!' The guards now encircled him, their spear points levelled at Harald's chest.

The new Emperor grew purple with rage. 'Impudent barbarian! Northern dog!' he bellowed. 'Take him to the dungeons and leave him to rot, and then, when he's good and ready, he will crawl in the dirt for forgiveness!'

———

But Harald would not beg for mercy. His experience in Christ's tomb had reminded him that he was a prince from beyond the north wind, and princes need ask forgiveness from neither gods nor men. Nor would the Emperor's threats and beatings break his spirit; instead he paced his cell in chains, plotting revenge.

As it turned out, he was not imprisoned for long – the new Emperor had miscalculated badly. The Empress could not be banished so easily, and Harald's own men would not leave him to rot.

One morning the door of Harald's cell burst inwards to reveal a horde of fierce Varangians determined to free their leader in the name of the true Empress. They shattered Harald's chains and returned his weapons to him. Then they knelt before him, calling him prince and warlord. Harald led them through the palace gardens, gathering supporters wherever he turned. He and his men fought fiercely with the Emperor's guardsmen on the steps of the Imperial Palace, but it was not long before the remainder had thrown down their weapons or fled.

The hapless Michael V was captured in the Imperial Treasury – caught stuffing his pockets with gemstones. The former Emperor's fate was grim. In later days Harald would tell anyone who would listen that it was he who had put out the Emperor's eyes, and it was easy to believe. But Harald was less cruel in his Varangian days than he was later to become, and most people thought the Empress had ordered that wicked deed.

Whatever the truth, Harald found himself in great favour with the Empress after those dramatic events and, for a time, he was content with the rewards and palaces he had; until, that is, a messenger arrived one day from the north.

The message he carried was to change everything.

The warrior

Being a warrior defined what it meant to be a Viking. For much of the Viking Age, men expressed their identities through elaborate weapons and distinctive armour. For pagan warriors, the greatest ambition was to die bravely in battle, as this would mean joining Odin in Valhalla to drink and feast until Ragnarok (see page 22). By Harald's day, beliefs about Valhalla were dying out. However, courageous deeds and a glorious death were still praiseworthy. Christian warriors could be remembered as martyrs and even saints. Viking warriors were feared and respected by the many peoples they came into contact with. They were highly valued as mercenaries and fought for the Byzantine Empire in the emperor's personal bodyguard: the Varangian Guard.

This axehead was found in Russia and the shape is typically Russian. It is decorated in silver with a Scandinavian style design on the blade. It would have belonged to a wealthy and powerful warrior.

This is a depiction of St Theodore from Constantinople, made around the time this story is set. It shows how warriors in the Byzantine Empire were armed and equipped.

The weapon that symbolized warrior status was the sword. Swords could be given names and would have been recognizable by their decorated hilts and scabbards.

The blade of this sword from Denmark has been made by a process called pattern-welding. When new, the polished steel would have looked like shimmering water.

Spears were the most common weapons of the Viking Age, but even these could be beautifully decorated, like this spearhead from Norway.

Some swords, like this one, have the name +VLFBERH+T (Ulfberht) on the blade. This was the name of a maker or workshop, similar to a modern brand logo. Blades of this type were typically made in the Rhineland (in modern Germany). The hilt, however, is from Scandinavia.

CHAPTER 4

Homecoming

 URING THE TIME *that Harald had been in Byzantium, fighting the Empire's wars, his nephew Magnus had grown to manhood. He was, in many ways, more a prince of the Rūs than a Norwegian. But he was still the son of Olaf the Saint and that counted for much. For in Norway the nobles had grown weary of Cnut, and when that great king died and left his English wife Ælfgifu and their useless son to rule the Norwegian lands, they decided they had had enough of Danish kings. And so messengers were sent to Yaroslav to ask whether the boy whose father had died a king at Stiklestad wanted to return to claim the throne. He did.*

Magnus made the journey west – the same journey Harald had made in the other direction – back to Norway to rule his father's realm.

This was the news that the messenger brought to Harald, and his fury was terrible to witness.

'How dare this runtling child call himself a king!' he raged. 'The boy barely blinked at the news of Olaf's death. Where was he when the king fell? Hiding with women and babies, and sucking on his thumb while I slew his enemies and suffered terrible wounds!'

The messenger grew pale and shrank against the wall.

'Tell me: what wars has he fought? How many foes has he slain? How many men can he command? Where is his fame? My name is known far and wide – the Bulgar-burner, the taker of cities! Kings and emperors have been felled by my hand! This will not stand!'

And Harald rushed away. Running up the steps of the Imperial Palace, he burst unannounced into the throne room where Zoe and her new husband, the Emperor Constantine IX, were holding court. They were annoyed at this rudeness, but Harald didn't care.

'Give me leave ... great lady ... lord ...' Harald was panting and red in the face with rage and excitement, 'to leave your service and travel north. I have word that my birthright has been usurped and I must leave at once to defend it!'

But the Empress Zoe was unmoved. She had never heard Harald talk about Norway or express any desire to return. After all, she had lavished treasures and palaces on him in reward for his loyalty and his many victories. So she refused him. Harald didn't argue, but spun on his heel and marched from the throne room without a word, his face set in a look of grim determination.

He summoned his hearth-companions – his closest comrades, many of whom had come with him from the north – and told them his plan. They'd fit out a ship, load it with as much treasure as they could carry and sail north – through the straits and into the Black Sea, and then up the Dnieper River to Kiev and the court of Yaroslav where they'd receive a royal welcome.

The plan nearly worked perfectly. Up the straits of the Bosphorus they rowed; the only sound was the slapping of oars in the dark velvet waters. Soon they would be away. But at that moment a cloud slipped from the moon's face and silver light struck the sea ahead. There in the water Harald saw the glint of iron. The chains! He realized in an instant that the Empress had known his thoughts. She had ordered the massive chains that stretched across the straits from shore to shore as a barrier against hostile ships to be raised.

But Harald didn't hesitate – he knew what fate awaited those who proved disloyal to the Empire.

'To your oars, men! Row as you have never rowed before!'

They sped towards the chains like an arrow through the night-dark sea. Suddenly they were upon them, the wooden keel of the ship grinding over the chains until the forward momentum of the ship was lost and it lurched, balanced halfway across. Harald ordered the men to run to the front of the ship and throw their weight into the prow. There was a terrible creaking and tearing as the vessel pitched forward. Suddenly, with a rush, it slid forward and they were away. The men rushed back to their oars and began to row again, swiftly northwards, towards the Black Sea.

Harald turned and looked back into the straits of the Bosphorus, at the water churning against those monstrous chains, and the fragments of torn timber that tossed in the swell. Farewell to blood and gold, he thought, as the light of the rising sun caught the gilded domes of Constantinople, staining them red against the purple sky.

———

Harald arrived in Kiev to great rejoicing and Yaroslav welcomed him as a long-lost son. Tales of his exploits and the evidence of his wealth had travelled up the rivers to Kiev and Novgorod for years, until Harald had become a figure of legend to the Rūs. The feast that Yaroslav prepared to welcome his return was lavish and memories of it lived long.

Harald told stories of his deeds and his adventures until the dawn, and all who heard him were amazed by his bravery and cunning. One who listened to him speak was a very beautiful young woman. She was noble and gracious, Harald thought, the sort of woman who might make a fine bride for a prince. The next day he asked Yaroslav who she was.

The Grand Prince smiled. 'Do you not remember? Last time you met her you treated her as one might an annoying pup! But she's never forgotten you, Harald. That's my daughter, Elisabeth.'

And Harald did remember the little girl with cow eyes who had followed him around at Novgorod. It seemed a lifetime ago.

'Great Prince,' said Harald, dropping at once to his knees, 'grant me her hand in marriage and I swear to make her a queen.'

Yaroslav laughed. 'Had you asked me this before you left I would have refused you, penniless refugee that you were.

But now you own wealth beyond any of my nobles and, if you intend to make yourself king by your own hand, and my daughter a queen, I don't doubt that you will. There is steel in you, Harald. I agree to your request, but you'd better ask Elisabeth if she'll have you!'

Elisabeth had loved Harald since she was a child, and the tales of his exploits had only made her all the more devoted to him (or, rather, to the idea of him, which isn't quite the same thing – as she would learn in later days). So she agreed to marry him with great joy, and the wedding festivities went on for several weeks. They were married in the cathedral of St Sophia in Kiev, a vast stone church that Yaroslav had begun to build after Harald had left for Constantinople. It was still not

complete, but already Harald saw that Yaroslav's dreams of that fabulous city were finding their form.

Harald and Elisabeth remained with Yaroslav for some time, but Harald was still anxious to return to Norway and confront his nephew, Magnus. Soon the time came when Elisabeth and Yaroslav could no longer keep him among the Rūs. At their parting Yaroslav bestowed many wondrous treasures on the couple, but none were as precious as the banner that he gave to Harald. On it was embroidered the image of a raven in flight.

'This is an heirloom of my house,' said the Grand Prince. 'None know for sure how it was made, but it's said that it was woven by three strange women, daughters of fate, and given to a king by a one-eyed wanderer. Maybe this is mere superstition; only God alone can say. But I know that, if the wind catches it up and the raven spreads its wings before battle, you will always be victorious. Landwaster is its name.'

Harald took the banner and it became his most closely guarded treasure.

———

There is no need to tell of the long farewells or of the journey from Yaroslav's lands through lakes and forests, rivers and seas. All of these things passed until one day Harald stood on the deck of his ship and saw, for the first time in fifteen years, the shores of Scandinavia – the land of his birth.

Harald, however, had not come in peace. He swiftly made contact with Svein Ulfsson, an old rival of Magnus, and began raiding the islands and coastlines. Much of Denmark, which Magnus claimed as part of his kingdom, submitted to Harald and Svein. Wherever coastal villages and towns were burned and pillaged, the dreaded banner Landwaster could be seen, the raven's wings spread wide amid the smoke of burning farmsteads. It was a bitter gift that Harald had brought back from his exile.

When Magnus heard that his uncle was intent on claiming the crowns of Norway and Denmark for himself, he was thrown into despair. He didn't want to fight his kinsman, even though they'd never known each other apart from that one brief meeting in Novgorod; and he was afraid of further bloodshed. Harald's reputation had travelled far beyond the lands of the Rūs and all knew that he was a fearsome warrior who would stop at nothing to get what he wanted.

Magnus sent messages in secret to Harald, promising to share the kingdom of Norway with him if he'd make peace, but Harald had no intention of sharing anything

with his young nephew. He was determined now to become king and, like everything he had achieved in his life, he would do it by the sword. That night, however, fate forced his hand.

There had been a quarrel. Svein had accused Harald of dishonouring his oaths and Harald had accused Svein of the same. These were terrible accusations among Viking men, and Harald sensed that their partnership would end badly. He had long had a good nose for treachery, and so he left a log in his bed that night and slept elsewhere. In the morning he found a huge axe embedded in the wood.

Harald woke his men. 'It's obvious,' he said, 'that we're in danger here, surrounded and outnumbered by Svein's men. It's clear that they plan to betray us so we must escape while we can.'

'Where shall we go, lord?' asked one of Harald's Vikings.

'To my kinsman, King Magnus.'

Harald was received with great dignity by his nephew Magnus. Both men disguised their feelings for each other and feasted together long into the night. Magnus bestowed rich gifts on Harald and his men, as was fitting from a king to a great lord, and eventually he offered Harald the greatest gift of all.

'I declare that you shall be lawfully joint-king with me over every part of Norway, and I give to you half of the land, together with all its wealth and taxes.'

Harald sprang to his feet, ready to accept this extraordinary offer.

'But,' Magnus fixed his uncle with a steely eye, 'whenever we are together, I shall be given precedence in greetings and in rank; I shall have the highest seat in hall; I will have the royal harbour whenever we are together. And you will support this kingdom and strengthen it in return for this gift.'

Harald's expression clouded. He wasn't used to being spoken to like this, but he had little alternative but to accept. It was, indeed, a generous offer. Harald would be a king, albeit subordinate to his nephew. He managed to control his temper. 'This is a great gift, Magnus, and I accept. It shall be as you say. And, what's more, you shall have half of the riches that I brought back with me from the east.' Harald knew full well that this was expected of him in return.

Magnus was happy. He had little wealth to compare with Harald's hoard of Byzantine gold and so both men got something they wanted from each other and things went well for a time between them. It was not long, however, before their differences came to the surface. Their meetings became fractious and disagreeable and they frequently argued. On one occasion Harald refused to move his ships from the royal jetty, and the two kings and their men nearly came to blows. Soon they couldn't bear to even be in each other's presence. Harald would rage about playing second fiddle to his nephew.

'What sort of king am I who must make way for a mere boy!'

But the trouble didn't last long. Magnus died, suddenly, at the age of only twenty-three. He was remembered as a great king by the people of Norway who called him Magnus the Good. His short life had been filled with adventures and deeds of bravery, all of which are tales for another day. Some say that his death was due to an accident; some say that it was the result of illness. All mourned his passing; all, that is, except two men: Svein Ulfsson was named on Magnus's deathbed as King of Denmark, Harald as King of Norway.

Now Harald was a true king and he would make way for no one.

But even this was not enough for him. He now felt that he was invincible and that all the north should bow down to him. Magnus had claimed the kingship of Denmark as well as Norway, and Harald wasted no time in turning his greedy eye towards that land. From the moment he was confirmed as sole King of Norway, Harald was at war with his former ally, King Svein.

———

Their wars were long and bloody. Many times Harald ravaged the coastline of Denmark, burning and plundering the settlements of his enemy. Over and over again he commanded levies of warriors to be called up from their farms to man his ships on expeditions south. Even his own people began to complain in private that Harald had become a tyrant, demanding obedience to his every whim. They didn't dare say so to his face, or even suggest alternatives to his plans. He had become ruthless, single-minded and obsessed with war.

It was at this time that Harald made use of the resources he had at his disposal to build himself a ship. He remembered the mighty ship built by his brother Olaf with forty pairs of oars and a terrible carved dragon that soared at its prow. It filled Harald's dreams. He had asked what had happened to it, but no one knew for certain. One old jarl said that it had been wrecked in Denmark at Roskilde Fjord and the timbers stripped from the hull to make houses for sailors. The thought of that made Harald angry and he decided that when his own ship was built he would use it to teach the Danes a lesson.

It was a magnificent vessel. A dragon's head reared up at the prow and a serpent's tail at the stern. Gold glinted all along the bows and in the carvings that ran all over the upper parts of the ship. As soon as it was finished, Harald challenged King Svein to meet him in battle and settle their dispute once and for all. The two kings assembled their fleets and met finally at the mouth of the River Niså.

Harald had 150 ships; King Svein had 300. Harald was outnumbered two to one, but these odds did not deter him. When some of his men suggested that they retreat,

he looked ahead grimly and
said,

'Better that we all lie dead in
heaps than run away.'

He ordered that the ships be
lashed together to form a solid
wall of timber, shields fixed
along the sides, and had his own
dragon-ship set in the centre
of the battle line. Fearlessly,
Harald faced his Danish foes
as they rushed forward to
attack.

The fighting raged all night
long and Harald stood for hours
firing arrows at the Danish ships.
Despite being outnumbered,
Harald's men were more
experienced warriors, and
eventually the Danish lines

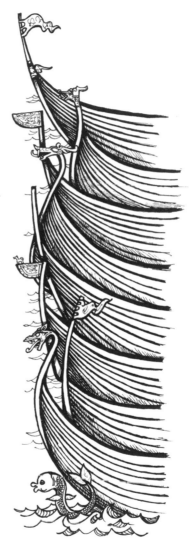

began to weaken. Towards morning, Harald sensed that the Danish army was close to collapse. Shouting for his closest comrades to follow him, he drew his sword and leapt across the gunwales on to the deck of King Svein's ship. The Norwegian Vikings were unstoppable, swinging their dreadful war axes and cleaving with their swords until all the Danish soldiers had been killed or driven overboard.

Harald was victorious once again, but his enemy – King Svein – had escaped him. He should have followed Svein to Denmark and made himself king there, crushing opposition and hunting down the survivors of the battle. Instead he began to hear troubling news, rumours that the farmers in the east of Norway were refusing to pay their taxes and planned to make another man – Earl Hakon Ivarsson – their lord.

Harald was furious, he knew that he had no choice but to return home. It would have done him little good to have conquered Denmark while losing his grip on the Norwegian throne. He could have ended up in Denmark as a king without a kingdom, surrounded by enemies in a hostile land. It was a bitter end to fifteen years of war with Svein, and it would be the farmers of Norway who would pay the price.

———

Harald sailed north. He met Earl Hakon's forces at Lake Varna, near the Swedish coast, and crushed them utterly. That winter he marched his army inland, relentless in his anger towards the upland farmers. It was bitingly cold, but Harald's rage seemed to keep him warm. Everywhere he marched – Hedmark, Hadeland, Ringerike – he burned the farms and killed the livestock, stripped men of their possessions and drove families out into the freezing winter.

Even this did not satisfy Harald; he was consumed with vengeance. At Romerike he had some of the wealthier farmers brought before him in front of a crowd of peasants. He ignored all their pleas for mercy. Some he killed outright; some he ordered to have their hands chopped off as punishment for supporting Earl Hakon's rebellion.

One man stood in the crowd, forced to watch these grim deeds, and was sure he recognized the king even though he hadn't seen him since Harald's return to Norway. The man was older than the king by a few years, a free peasant who had a farm near the border with the land of the Swedish king. His father had died and left him the little farmstead a few years earlier. He looked down and saw the silver ring he wore around his arm. Suddenly he remembered where he had met Harald before. He'd been only a young man guiding a frightened youth through the forest to the Swedish king's hall. He remembered the verses the boy had spoken:

'Now I pass from wood to wood,
A wanderer of little worth;
Who knows? My name may yet be
Known far and wide hereafter.'

He said to himself,

'Now you are king, who was once a friendless exile. And you'll be famous indeed. But men will remember you as a cruel king, Harald Hard-ruler.'

Power

Powerful Vikings displayed their wealth by wearing it. The silver and gold that came from successful raids and trading missions could be converted into intricately crafted jewellery and ornamented weapons, and Viking art was highly sophisticated. Kings and other rulers could also display their power in different ways. Churches, halls and especially warships consumed vast quantities of timber, wool (for sails and tapestries) and precious metals. The ability to control and spend such resources showed how rich and influential a particular ruler was. By the end of the Viking age, kings like Harald could command huge numbers of men and build substantial fleets of ships.

Brooches like this would have been worn by men to fasten their cloaks, and were popular with Vikings around the Irish Sea. Some brooches of this sort are enormous and would have been very impractical, but would have marked out their owners as wealthy individuals.

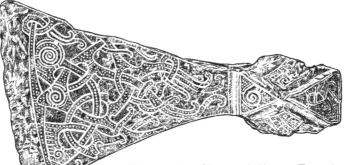

This axe is from Mammen in Norway. The surface is covered all over with serpent-like animals inlaid in silver. Warriors wanted to be recognized as wealthy and powerful, and there was no better way to do this than through decorated weapons.

Wealthy Viking women showed off their status with beautiful jewellery. This brooch is of a type that was particularly popular on the island of Gotland.

Rings for arms and fingers were symbolic of wealth. A generous King could be described as a 'ring-giver' and would distribute gold and silver rings to his followers.

This is one of a number of gold pendants found in a hoard of treasure in northern Germany. The craftsmanship is very beautiful and shows how sophisticated Viking art could be.

CHAPTER 5

Invasion

 HE WAR *with Denmark was over. Harald would never be king of all Scandinavia as he had hoped. He was old for a warrior – nearly fifty – which was a ripe old age in those days. Despite his brutality in dealing with rebellious subjects, in other ways he had tried to be a good king. He remembered dishonest Leifr and his suspect weights and so had silver coins made to help people trade their goods fairly. He also used his contacts to encourage trade with Byzantium and many wondrous things came to Norway in his day that had not been much seen in the north before.*

Most of all he tried to follow the example of his father-in-law, Yaroslav, by building churches and bringing priests from the east. He was successful and the Christian faith grew strong in Norway under his rule. He even founded a new city at Oslo where he built his royal hall. But no one talked of him as they spoke of Yaroslav the Wise, or even of his late nephew Magnus the Good, who was loved in memory by all the Norwegian people. All they saw of Harald was his harsh justice and his fierce temper: Hardrada – 'hard-ruler' – they called him behind his back.

This made him angry, and then he'd lash out and commit some terrible deed, and people would whisper that he was a violent and vengeful king. Even his wife, Elisabeth, had grown more distant over the years. He had frequently been away from home on campaigns, and when he was at home all he would talk about was war and killing. She was often appalled by his violence and his foul moods, and she preferred to spend time with the Greek monks she had invited to Norway. So, lonely and bitter, he would sulk on his throne and brood on days of glory gone by: of how he'd been the terror of the enemies of Byzantium, the Bulgar-burner, the scourge of the

Pechenegs. Then he would remember how he had lost the throne of Denmark and how Svein Ulfsson still ruled there … and was popular too, more popular than Harald had ever been.

————

One day a man called Audun arrived at Harald's hall. He had brought with him a wonderful marvel, a creature that few had ever seen and a legend among the people of the north. It was a great white bear, bigger even than the most enormous bear in Norway's forests. It was so big that it only just got through the door. Audun said that he'd bought it in Greenland for everything he owned. Harald was much taken with it. He liked the idea of owning a giant white bear. That would be something to rub in Svein's face.

'I'll give you what you paid for this bear,' Harald told Audun.

'No thank you,' answered the man.

'Well – what if I give you double what you paid?' Harald

suggested, slightly crossly.

'No. I don't want to.'

'So why don't you give it to me then?' Harald was clearly irritated now. How dare this little man refuse him anything?

'No, lord, I won't. I want to take it to King Svein as a gift.'

Harald went red in the face. This was not what he'd wanted to hear at all.

'Svein!' he bellowed. 'Are you so stupid that you haven't heard about our wars? What's to stop me taking your bear and doing what I like with you?'

'Nothing can stop you, lord. I'm just telling you what I want to do. I gave up all I owned to buy this bear and make this trip.'

Harald clenched his fists and grimaced. He wanted to make an example of this foolish man, but he knew that his people would think even more badly of him than they already did.

'So be it,' he finally said through clenched teeth. 'Go and see Svein. But come back and tell me what he gave you for it.'

Audun did come back. In return for the gift of the bear, Svein had given him high honours, a ship filled with goods, a sack of silver and a beautiful arm-ring so that, if all else was lost, he would still have something to show for the gift of the great white bear. None of this pleased Harald. It was much more than he would have given, and Audun even managed to make him feel slightly ashamed by giving him the arm-ring in gratitude for his safe passage. Harald felt obliged to give Audun a few gifts in exchange, but this didn't stop people whispering that he was a miserly king compared to Svein Ulfsson.

So it was, despite all he had achieved, that Harald was an unhappy ruler. He was bored. He was restless. His whole life had been devoted to war, and now he spent most of his time sitting around doing nothing. Out of frustration he would sometimes set off on dangerous expeditions. On one occasion he took a ship to the far north of his kingdom, to lands which hardly anyone had ever seen before.

Towering mountains of ice floated upon the frigid sea, rearing up in strange shapes, and weird ribbons of green light would flicker and bend across the night sky. Harald remembered tales of the frost giants who lived beyond the rim of the world and wondered whether he might be close to their realm. It was a dangerous road, where ships could be lost on the grinding ice sheets, and to fall into the water meant certain death. Only by retracing his course did Harald return alive, and even then the terrible storms of the far north nearly claimed him. After that, he didn't attempt any more dangerous journeys.

———

One day another stranger arrived in Harald's hall. He was a foreigner from a land beyond the sea, an Anglo-

Saxon from England. His name was Tostig and he was the brother of the English King Harold Godwinson. Tostig had once been a powerful lord, the Earl of Northumbria in the north of England, but the people there had turned against him (they accused him of being greedy and high-handed). His brother, King Harold, had taken the earldom from him and sent him into exile where he'd licked his wounds and plotted how he might return and claim the throne of England for himself. Finally he'd come up with a plan, and had come to Oslo to enlist the help of the Norwegian King – who everyone knew was the most fearsome warrior in the whole of Europe.

Tostig stood before the high seat in Harald's hall. He was a slightly built man with a noble bearing. His chin was clean-shaven, but his moustache was long and drooping in the Anglo-Saxon fashion. The king leant forwards and asked him why he had come.

'I have a question for you, Harald Hard-ruler.' Harald flinched at the name, but Tostig carried on. 'How is it that such a great king as you couldn't hold on to Denmark as your nephew Magnus did?'

Harald's courtiers looked at one another nervously and started to shuffle towards the door. They couldn't begin to imagine how Harald would react to such an insult. But Harald sat calmly and showed no reaction, even though he regularly had men beaten (and worse) for lesser insults.

'What's your point? I've given those Danes a good hiding often enough.' he said gruffly.

'The point, great lord, is that if the people of Denmark had wanted you as king – as they wanted Magnus – you would have met no resistance there.'

'So?' said Harald, starting to look menacing, 'Tell me what you want, Englander, or I'll throw you out and make sure you have a rough landing.'

'Well … you spent fifteen years trying to conquer that land without success. But imagine if another land was crying out for you as their rightful king and you would simply have to reach out your hand to take it.'

These words made Harald pay closer attention to the man in front of him.

'What land would yield itself to me so readily?' he asked.

'England,' said Tostig. 'Did you know that Magnus also claimed the throne of that land?' he asked.

'Yes, I did, but he was too cowardly to take it for himself.'

Tostig shook his head.

'He knew that the people there didn't want him, just as the Danes don't want you. But the English are now desperate for a strong Viking warlord to be their king, as Cnut the Great was. Everyone knows that you're the greatest ruler in the world and, if you trust me, I promise that all the people of England will support you and rejoice at your arrival.'

Harald sat back in his throne and thought about this. Maybe it wasn't so far-fetched. It was true that England was full of people descended from Norwegians and Danes who might prefer a Viking king to a Saxon one. And it was also true that the kings of Norway had some claim over the lands ruled by Cnut, and that Viking kings had ruled in many parts of England in the past. He thought of old Eric Bloodaxe, who had ruled in Northumbria before Harald was born. Great tales were told of that king – of how he had died in battle and been taken to Valhalla to sit by Odin's side, feasting and fighting until the end of the world.

Harald smiled to himself: the pagans had a good afterlife and he hoped heaven would be like that, not full of chanting monks. He began to imagine the feel of the sword in his hand, the creak of the ship's timbers and the din of battle. He thought of raising Landwaster aloft over foreign shores and seeing the fear in the eyes of his enemies. Before he knew it he was on his feet, the blood pumping through his limbs. He felt the weight of years slipping from his shoulders,

'Yes … YES! That would be a fine adventure!' he shouted. 'I've sat and rotted here for far too long!' He glared at his earls. 'Why does it take an English exile to put the fire

back into my belly? You dogs would've been happy to watch me grow old and fat! No chance of that … Harald Sigurdsson will go to war again, thanks to Tostig son of Godwin, and together we will spill the blood of many an Anglo-Saxon!'

––––––––

The fleet was assembled and it was an awesome sight. The sea was black with ships from horizon to horizon, all bristling with the weapons of warriors, shields gleaming on the gunwales, dragon heads rearing up below the sails. Harald was pleased and he felt a new energy. Making arrangements for the campaign, speaking to the soldiers, being on board ship … these things made him feel alive, and for the first time in years he was happy. He was a warrior king and this was what he had been born to do. He hoped his brother Olaf would be proud.

But among the men there were dark murmurings, and people whispered that the omens weren't good. Men dreamt terrible dreams of a fearsome troll-witch who rode on a monstrous wolf. She stood on the shoreline devouring corpses, one after another, blood streaming

over the sand. In the distance a shadowy army stood,
banners flying in the unnatural wind.

'The troll-witch sees the doom awaiting Harald,' she
shrieked. 'Her claws rend the flesh of dead warriors; the
wolf's greedy jaws are stained with gore. Carrion
birds follow you, sea-king. They know that
England's graveyards will soon be filled
with the dead!'

Stories of these dreadful dreams spread throughout Harald's army, casting a gloomy atmosphere aboard the ships. Harald didn't seem to notice: he was too busy and excited preparing for the invasion.

————

It all started well enough. The fleet sailed for Shetland and then Orkney, islands north of Britain that had long been Viking colonies. There Harald was joined by the sons of Thorfinn the Mighty, the fearsome Earl of Orkney. From there they sailed to Cleveland, and the people fled before him: none dared to resist. Then the fleet reached Scarborough and there the Vikings fought with the English and burned the town to the ground. After that, the survivors bent the knee to Harald and acknowledged him as their lord. At Holderness some local soldiers arrived to offer resistance to Harald's army. They too were utterly defeated, and so it went on.

Everywhere Harald went the people submitted to him, and before long a huge area north of the Humber was in his grip. His mood was light and jovial – he could see now that Tostig knew the situation in England well.

Everything had been just as he'd promised it would be. Never had Harald imagined that winning such a great kingdom could be so easy. The mood among the men lightened as well. The grim omens were forgotten as the loot of pillaged English towns began to mount up. Nothing banished dark thoughts so quickly as treasure easily won.

The first real battle came when Harald sailed into the mouth of the Humber and up the River Ouse. There an English host had assembled on the shore, ready to face him, led by the Earls Edwin and Morcar. They were two of the most powerful warlords in England and had brought a large army of Anglo-Saxon warriors from York to face the Vikings.

It was not enough. Harald raised Landwaster high and stormed into the English lines. Nothing could stand before that furious charge, so fierce was Harald and so confident his warriors. The English scattered and tried to flee. Many men fell attempting to cross the dykes and marshes until, it was said, the Vikings were able to walk on a bridge of corpses to avoid wetting their feet in the swamp. Edwin and Morcar retreated and the people of York sent their submission to the Norwegian king. Now, Harald thought, all of northern England was in his grasp and no one could oppose him.

He was wrong.

———

The next day Harald set out with some chosen men for York. It was warm and the sun was shining brightly. Harald decided that they should leave their armour at the ships and set out in a boisterous mood. He was feeling confident and pleased with the prospect of his new kingdom – it seemed greener and more fertile than any land he'd seen in all his travels. He pictured himself riding with a hawk at his wrist, hunting boar in the wild woods and building a magnificent hall.

They came to a bridge over a river. Harald wondered what sort of fish might be caught here – he had enjoyed fishing in his idle hours. Tostig told the king that this was the River Derwent, and the bridge was called Stamford Bridge. Suddenly, they saw in the distance riders on the horizon; mail shirts shone white, the dust of horses rose in a great cloud and banners billowed black against the bright blue sky. It was a mighty host arrayed for war, their weapons glittering and sparkling like broken ice in the morning sun.

'What is this?' Harald turned to Tostig with a grim look in his eye. Tostig didn't answer, but his face grew tight and drawn.

Harald ordered runners to send word back to the ships to bring the armour and reinforcements. It seemed that the fighting wasn't over after all.

A group of riders came up from the army that was assembling into its battle formation. They carried the banners of their warlords – the standards of Earls Edwin and Morcar and another, greater than the others. On it was the image of an armed warrior, a fighting man. The group approached the place where Harald and Tostig stood and their leader addressed Tostig:

'King Harold Godwinson, King of the English, sends his

greetings to Earl Tostig. He offers peace and forgiveness and the return of his lands if the earl will give up this folly and rejoin the English.'

Tostig looked disdainful. 'These are fine sentiments from the king, but where were they last winter when I was hounded out of England like a wolf? Many men are now dead who need not be, and England is in a sorry state thanks to him!'

He hesitated. 'And if I was to accept this offer what compensation would the king offer to my friend Harald of Norway, who has come all this way at great labour and expense?'

The rider unsheathed his sword and pointed it at the ground in front of them.

'King Harold Godwinson will grant the King of Norway this: seven feet of English ground or as much as it takes to lay him in it.'

But Tostig was defiant: 'Go then, and make ready for

the storm of spears and the clash of shields; Tostig Godwinson will not abandon his ally, and neither of us shall leave this land until it is conquered or we both lie dead upon the field.'

Harald didn't understand the English language that they spoke, but he sensed the tone of the exchange and reached for his sword. But the rider spurred his horse and was gone, back to the English lines with his companions. They heard the horns blowing as the English forces made ready to advance.

'Who was that man?' asked Harald, pulling on his helmet and picking up his shield.

'That was Harold Godwinson, King of England,' Tostig replied; he showed no trace of emotion in his voice.

'If I had revealed him, you'd surely have killed him. But he's my brother and he offered me a generous peace. I'd rather he was my killer than I his.'

Harald looked at Tostig in amazement, but said no more.

The Norwegians and Tostig's men formed their battle lines, and Harald raised Landwaster so his men could see where the king fought and draw courage from the battle standard. But the wind had died and the flag hung limp against the pole. If Harald noticed, he said nothing – there was no time to worry about prophecy: the battle was about to begin.

It was in the clash of shield walls that the fighting would be decided; swords, spears and axes hewed, cleaved and stabbed until shield was shattered and helmet sundered. The dead piled up around the feet of the living until warriors tripped and fell over their slain comrades only to be speared to death where they lay in the mud. Soon the green fields were churned to a muddy wreck, slick with blood and littered with broken weapons and armour.

Harald sensed that this deadlock would not easily be broken, and that – without armour and outnumbered – his men would eventually dwindle until their resistance was broken. He couldn't wait for reinforcements to arrive from the ships, so he made up his mind to lead one last charge deep into the heart of the enemy. He hefted his sword in one hand and his axe in another – his shield now long forgotten – and hurled himself into the English, bellowing his war cry.

Nothing could withstand him: no helmet or coat of mail offered protection against the fury of his charge. The Norwegians followed in his wake, hacking and stabbing all who opposed them in a berserk frenzy. The English fell back, unable to withstand the Viking assault. And it was then, at the point of victory, that Harald fell.

He was struck by an arrow that pierced his throat and, though he snapped off the shaft and tried to fight on, the strength was leaving him. The sword slipped from his fingers and he sank down to the soft earth. Harald heard the English give up a great shout and knew that, with him gone, the tide of battle would turn against his army. Somewhere above him he heard Tostig cry out and sensed him fall. All around him his closest companions, the warriors of his hearth, fought on. All of them, to a man, would die with their king: not one would bow their heads to a strange lord; not one would beg for mercy.

Harald lay where he had fallen and looked up into the darkening sky as two ravens circled above him. The noise of battle faded away, until all he could hear was the sound of waves crashing on faraway shores. As the sun began to sink into the dim and distant west, Harald smiled. It was a good way to die, he thought: a warrior's death – a Viking death. Olaf would be proud.

He closed his eyes. Somewhere above him he thought he heard hoof-beats in the wind and saw, in his mind's eye, a shimmer of rainbow-coloured light. He thought he glimpsed his brother's face caught in a golden glow and called out to him. But the figure moved off and suddenly Harald was walking towards a great gate from which came the sounds of music and warm laughter. He reached the door and entered, and was gone.

EPILOGUE

Harald died at Stamford Bridge along with many of the warriors who accompanied him to England. It was said that fifty years after the battle a traveller to the north could still see the whitening bones of Harald's army, left where they had fallen on the field at Stamford Bridge. A year later, Harald's son, Olaf, would return to reclaim his bones and take them back to Norway where they were buried.

Never again would a Viking warlord come so close to conquering England. Within a couple of generations Scandinavian warriors were more likely to be found on a crusade in the Holy Land than raiding the settlements of their Christian neighbours, as they had in earlier centuries.

Harold Godwinson had little time to celebrate his victory over the Vikings. Two weeks later, he too was dead, killed by the Normans at the Battle of Hastings. The Viking Age was over. A new age – an age of knights, castles and crusades – was about to begin.

Raiders and conquerors

From 787 when the first recorded Viking raid on Britain took place, to 1066 when Harald invaded England, Viking fleets menaced the coastline of Britain and Ireland. At first these were small-scale attacks on undefended monasteries and settlements. Over time, however, the number of ships increased and the ambitions of Viking war bands grew. Vikings established kingdoms and earldoms throughout Britain and Ireland. By the 890s they had conquered huge areas of northern and eastern England, a region that came to be known as the 'Danelaw'. Eventually, the whole of England came to be ruled by Viking kings – first by Svein Forkbeard and then by his son, Cnut the Great. It was the speed, strength and manoeuvrability of the Viking ship that made these raids and conquests possible.

This cross was raised in Yorkshire, England, at a time when it was ruled by Viking kings. It shows a Viking warrior equipped for battle.

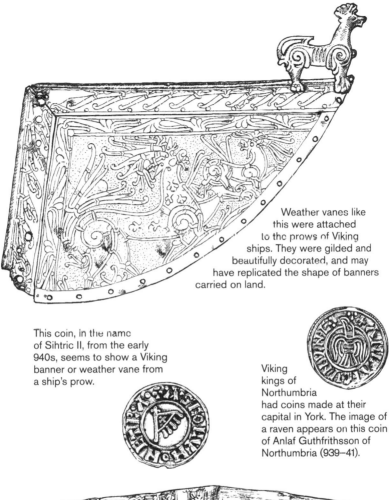

Weather vanes like this were attached to the prows of Viking ships. They were gilded and beautifully decorated, and may have replicated the shape of banners carried on land.

This coin, in the name of Sihtric II, from the early 940s, seems to show a Viking banner or weather vane from a ship's prow.

Viking kings of Northumbria had coins made at their capital in York. The image of a raven appears on this coin of Anlaf Guthfrithsson of Northumbria (939–41).

Although this stick from Bergen in Norway was carved after the Viking Age (in the late 1200s), it helps to show us what a fleet of Scandinavian ships would have looked like. The dragon heads and weather vanes are clearly depicted.

A note on the saga

The Tale of King Harald is a true story...

But what does it mean for a story to be 'true'? The first versions were recorded in the middle ages in hand-written texts. The oldest of these was compiled around 1220 in a manuscript called *Morkinskinna*, which means 'mouldy skin' (the parchment it was written on was made of vellum, made from the stretched and dried skin of a calf). The most famous version was written by an Icelandic chieftain and historian called Snorri Sturluson around 1230. Snorri was a remarkable man. As well as twice being elected to Iceland's highest official post – Lawspeaker (*Lögsögumaður*) – he wrote a number of works about traditional Scandinavian poetry and mythology, and also a compendium of Kings' Sagas (tales) called *Heimskringla* ('the circle of the world'). *Harald's Saga* forms a small part of this great work. Snorri was very careful to present what he thought were true accounts of the lives of the kings of Norway. He made great use of earlier histories, like *Morkinskinna*, and included fragments of poems (called skaldic verse) written during the lifetime of the kings, and remembered long afterwards.

In the case of King Harald, we have a little more to go on. He was mentioned in histories written in the Byzantine Empire where he was described as a Varangian with a prominent rank in the imperial army. His invasion of England is also described in the Anglo-Saxon Chronicle. So we know he existed, and the broad outlines of his life as presented by Snorri seem more or less accurate. However, poems in praise of kings are rarely even-handed, and some of the details seem improbable and rather similar to folk-tales told about other kings. It is telling that some

A NOTE ON THE SAGA

of the stories sound like boastings of a man in later life about the glories of his youth, at a time when no one could contradict his version of events. If this is so, we can expect some of these stories to contain a degree of exaggeration.

This version of Harald's story is fairly true to the account in *Heimskringla*. In some places I have added details taken from earlier sagas, especially *Saint Olaf's Saga* (the tale of Harald's half-brother who died at the Battle of Stiklestad). The tale of Audun and the polar bear is taken from a short story preserved in *Morkinskinna*, and a few details have been added from other sources that mention Harald and the period in general. Much of the dialogue is adapted from the saga, but by no means all of it. The biggest changes I have made are to the length of various sections of the narrative. In *Heimskringla* Harald's time with Yaroslav is told on a single page; therefore much of chapter 2 has been fleshed out with details of the period taken from other sources. On the other hand, chapters 3 and 4 present a greatly compressed version of Snorri's story-telling – in particular, the politics of Norway and Denmark during Harald's reign have been simplified.

I don't think Harald would have minded these minor changes. It was important for a Viking to live long in memory; I am sure he would be pleased that his legend continues to be told.

King Harald's Saga is available from Penguin Classics in a modern English translation by Magnus Magnusson and Hermann Pálsson.

A note from the author

I can still recall my excitement when I discovered, as a child, that Viking
warriors had lived, fought and died throughout Britain. I devoured
stories by Terry Jones and Henry Treece and retellings of the Norse
Myths by Roger Lancelyn-Green and others. The world they described
seemed strange and remote compared to the more familiar Greek and
Roman tales, but also closer at hand on the grey and misty mornings
of a childhood spent in Northern Europe. I was particularly fascinated
by the tale of King Harald Hard-ruler – who had scuppered (so it was
taught to me at school) the English resistance to the Normans at the
battle of Hastings in 1066. It was much later that I discovered what an
extraordinary life that Norwegian King had led. It is a life that deserves
to be more than a mere footnote to the familiar story of the Norman
Conquest.

This book would not have been possible without the help of others.
My wife Zeenat Williams has shown great patience with the late nights
and endless talk of bloody deeds in strange lands. Gareth Williams has
provided invaluable advice and encouragement. Claudia Bloch, through
her advocacy and hard work, has been instrumental in seeing this book
through to completion. The greatest debt is to my parents who, aside
from sparking my original enthusiasm for the Viking Age, have been
actively involved in producing this book. My father, Geoffrey Williams,
has provided a great deal of support, as well as an unerring critical eye.

It has been a joy to work so closely with my mother, Gilli Allan, on the
illustrations. Her artwork speaks for itself. My gratitude to her is as
profound as my delight with the results.